Siblings

A Story of A Family In Hong Kong

WILLIAM FUNG

Order this book online at www.trafford.com
or email orders@trafford.com

Most Trafford titles are also available at major online book retailers.

Printed in the United States of America.

ISBN: 978-1-4669-9311-2 (sc)
ISBN: 978-1-4669-9313-6 (hc)
ISBN: 978-1-4669-9312-9 (e)

Library of Congress Control Number: 2013907886

Trafford rev. 05/03/2013

Trafford
PUBLISHING®   www.trafford.com

North America & international
toll-free: 1 888 232 4444 (USA & Canada)
phone: 250 383 6864 ♦ fax: 812 355 4082

CONTENTS

PREFACE

The book "Siblings" tells the story about the struggle of a Chinese family during the pre- and postwar years in Hong Kong. Based on recollections of the author and his two older brothers, the author wrote about how his eldest brother had started from nothing to become a successful entrepreneur and how he took care of his sister and younger brothers in a subtle way by helping them in their lives, their families, and their careers.

The book covers more than a half century of events about the family in the tiny city of Hong Kong. As Hong Kong grew from a poor British colony into a thriving city and an important financial centre, the family also prospered. The children of *Siblings* are now living in Hong Kong, Taiwan, North America, Europe, and Australia. The author of the book is the youngest son, and to express his gratitude towards his siblings, especially his eldest brother, he wrote this book as a token of appreciation and honour to him.

With the book, the author is hoping that the offspring will learn about their roots, but more importantly, the special relationship and bond between siblings. The author used his Chinese name *Sin* (善) throughout the book, as this is the name he is called at home by his parents and siblings. The names of the family members and names of places in Hong Kong are real.

Thanks to Kwan Tsui and Raymond for providing the data and information related to the materials of the book, without their support, it would be impossible to write and publish the story about the family.

Thanks to Felix, Cindy, and Stephanie for their editorial assistance in shaping this book.

Finally, I like to thank Karen for her patience and understanding while I was writing this book.

CHAPTER ONE

A Family Gathering in Hong Kong

S in (善) was very excited to fly to Hong Kong to begin his Asian tour. Karen and Sin only took a few days to plan out this trip, the original idea to have this tour was instigated by Sin, and, she as usual, agreed to the plan with a mild objection on the return date. She preferred to return later than November 11th, 2012, so that she could stay in Hong Kong longer and maybe take another all-inclusive land tour in the region. Being retired they surely could afford the time, but Sin had to return to Canada to fulfill an obligation. He was required to attend the AGM on November 12th, as he is a director of the board of the Condominium Corporation of the apartment building in which Sin and Karen reside.

In the last five years, Sin travelled to Hong Kong on four occasions prior to this one. Of those four trips, two of which were to attend weddings, the third was traveling to China for the Yangtze River tour, and the trip in 2008 was sadly for attending the funeral of his sister, Yun (潤), the oldest sibling of the family.

A couple of days before flying to Hong Kong, Sin called long distance to his second elder brother Foo (富) and asked him to arrange a family gathering dinner on the night of their arrival on October 16th. He wanted to see his siblings and their families in Hong Kong whenever there was an opportunity. Sin figured that the itinerary for him and Karen would be quite busy and aggressive for this Asian tour, which began from October 18th to November 3rd. The tour included a six-day cruise on the Royal Caribbean International's Legend of the Seas to Sanya (China) and Vietnam's Danang and Ha Long Bay; followed by a flight (after disembarkation at Hong Kong) to Thailand for a six-day package land tour of Bangkok and Pattaya; and then another five-day package land tour of Guilin and Yangshuo, China; with only a two-night stay in Hong Kong between Thailand and Guilin to wash their dirty clothes. Sin thought that it would be strategically safer to plan ahead and to have the dinner gathering first before all the tours began.

At the end of the sixteen hour non-stop flight to Hong Kong, Sin and Karen dragged their tired bodies and luggage from the arrival hall to the Citybus terminal at the Hong Kong International Airport. Sin has made his home in Toronto, Canada, since 1968, and visiting Hong Kong is quite challenging because the city has changed so much. Thanks to the advent of the internet, before the journey Sin had searched for the information he needed regarding public transportation at the HKG International airport. At a cost of less than US$5.00 each, Sin and Karen took a relaxing ride on the Route

A21 bus that transported them from the airport to Tsim Sha Tsui, Kowloon. On Nathan Road, they got off the bus near the doorstep of the hotel where they had booked to stay for two nights. After checking in, Sin called Foo from the hotel room to inform him of their arrival and received confirmation from him that their dinner gathering would be at 6:00 p.m.

When Sin and Karen showed up at the restaurant in Mong Kok, Kowloon, Foo and his wife Tse Gam Ching (謝鑑清) were there to greet them. To Sin's surprise, the gathering was a celebration arranged by his brother for his newborn grandson. It is a common custom for the Chinese to celebrate the arrival of a newborn by inviting close relatives and friends to attend a banquet dinner on the newborn's 30th day birthday. Well, it turned out that his grandson was not quite 30 days old yet, but Foo took the opportunity to have the dinner reception moved ahead a few days to coincide with Sin's arrival. Sin felt very much appreciated for what Foo had planned. Anyway, the reception was a pleasant surprise for Sin only expected a smaller gathering. Sin knows that whenever his older brothers plan to meet for dinner, they prefer to have V.S.O.P. or X.O. brandies on the table, so he brought with him the bottle he bought from the duty-free liquor store at the Toronto International Airport prior to boarding.

A while later in the evening, Sin's eldest brother Keung (強) arrived at the restaurant with his family as well as other members of Foo's family and many other guests. The dinner party was about forty people in total, Sin was delighted that Keung's second daughter Wai Yan (慧茵) and son-in-law Kwan Tsui (徐鋃); son Raymond (禮民) and daughter-in-law Peggy; and youngest daughter Margaret (慧明) were at the party. Raymond and Peggy were vacationing in Hong Kong at that time and were scheduled to go back to Australia the day after, so it was a nice surprise to see them again in Hong Kong after attending their wedding a year before. Foo's older son Jackson (禮信) and middle grandson Toby (天佑), daughters-in-law Rita (Jackson's wife) and Ally (Benny's wife), middle daughter Freda (慧敏) and son-in-law C.W. Luk (陸志偉), were also at the party. Foo's oldest grandson Hugo Luk (陸嘉聰) was studying in the U.S. and was not present at the party.

Foo's youngest son Benny (禮邦), the father of the newborn, commuted back to Hong Kong from his job in Guangzhou for this dinner. Benny told Sin that his baby son's name is *Long Hin* (朗軒), and coincidentally, on June 1st, 2012, Sin's grandson was born and Sin had picked *Long Yin* (朗然) as his Chinese name. *Long Yin* is the Romanization or Cantonese way of "spell-out sound" for 朗然. Sin picked this Chinese name 朗然 because the character 朗 is compatible with those who are born in the year of the dragon. The character 朗 in Chinese means clear (as in clear voice, 朗聲; or as in clear sky, 天朗). The Mandarin way of "spell-out sound" or pinyin (the official system to transcribe Chinese characters into Latin script) for the Chinese character 龍 (meaning dragon) is *long*. (Two Chinese dialects are used here to explain the "spell-out sound" for the Chinese characters 朗 and 龍; the phonetic for 朗 in Cantonese is *long*, and the phonetic for 龍 in Mandarin is also *long*.)

CHAPTER TWO

An Idea to Write a Book about the Family

After exchanging of pleasantries, the three brothers and family members gathered together to take a group photo. The last time the three brothers (強,富,善) and their eldest sister Yun, were posing in the same photograph was in October of 2007 in Hong Kong.

The restaurant servers had just served the dinner's third course; Sin was feeling very pleasant but a bit light-headed, maybe due to the combined effects of jetlag, the lack of sleep for over twenty-four hours, and the alcohol he consumed from the brandy. All three brothers, Keung, Foo, and Sin were at the same table. After a few rounds of brandy (and yes, Chinese like to have brandy during the meal), the subject of conversation would automatically be related to the old days, talking about back when how things were, and what events happened around such times and places. Occasionally, Keung and Foo would disagree on the calendar year for certain events that were being brought up. It was fun to listen to them, and it was all nostalgic when the three brothers reminisced. It was a challenge to try to recall some events that happened seventy or eighty years ago! Then an idea flashed across Sin's cerebrum. Why not having these events written down in a book?

Sin was thinking of writing a book about the family but he didn't say it out loud at the table. Keung is the eldest male of the *fong* (房) that represents the lineage that can be traced back to his great grandfather. Keung and his siblings are fourth generation, counting from the great grandfather. The great grandfather had four sons and a daughter. However, in old China, only the male descendants were counted in the blood line, therefore there were four *fongs*, linkages or branches that originated from the great grandfather. Sin's grandfather was one of the four sons. Sin was thinking that writing a book about his family, and including stories about his grandfather and great grandfather if possible, would be a good idea in educating the younger generations after him. It would not be an easy task though, due to the fact that Sin is the youngest of the siblings, and he was born after the grandfather had passed away, and knows very, very little about the grandfather, and least about the great grandfather. It's unfortunate both Keung and Foo do not know the names of their grandfather and great grandfather, and there aren't any living family relatives around to provide any information. Sin wishes that his sister is still alive because she might remember some stories related to their father and about their lives in Hong Kong during its occupation by the Japanese. She was the eldest of the siblings and during the War she stayed in Hong

Kong and spent more time with their father, while the rest of the siblings were with their mother in China. It is logical to assume that her father would have told her stories related to their grandfather and great grandfather.

Sin was still determined to write the book about the family; he was able to obtain information from Keung and Foo and begin with his father's life story. Therefore Sin thought of approaching Keung's son-in-law, Kwan Tsui, after the tour to talk to him about the book idea. Sin supposed that Kwan Tsui would be the best candidate to help him obtain information from Keung about him and the family, because they live in the same part of the world, where as, Sin is half the world away in Canada. The second motive for Sin to write the book was that being the youngest child he received a greater share of love and care from his siblings; he thought there was no better way to express his gratitude to them than to use words in a book.

After dinner, Sin was totally exhausted from the effects of a long flight and the eating of a ten-course meal which is typical in a Chinese banquet. The book idea was still in Sin's head though, despite of all this. However, Sin would put this idea temporarily in his back pocket because in the next eighteen days, Sin and Karen would be on their tour. He planned to start writing the book after he had finished traveling and returned home to Canada.

CHAPTER THREE

A Humble Beginning for the Family

In 1932, Japan occupied Manchuria in northern China and established the puppet state of Manchukuo. Sin did not know why his parents were living in Hong Kong instead of staying in China. It was probably dreading the possibility of Japanese invasion into the southern part of China that made them decide to immigrate to Hong Kong in 1933. The family initially lived on Tai Nan Street, Kowloon, and about five years later in 1938, the family moved to the shantytown on Nam Cheong Street, Sham Shui Po. Late in 1941, their lives were once again affected by the Japanese aggression.

The Japanese military launched a series of attacks on Pearl Harbour, Northern Malaysia, the Philippines, Guam, Wake Island and

Hong Kong. On the 25th of December 1941, Hong Kong surrendered to the Empire of Japan. As a result, in the spring of 1942, the entire family left Hong Kong for Macao which was a neutral Portuguese port in South China. Sin's father thought that the family would be safer in Macao; however this neutrality did not last long because the Japanese converted Macao into a virtual Japanese protectorate.

After staying in Macao for about half a year, Sin's father decided that his wife and their two sons should leave Macao, while he moved back to Hong Kong with his daughter Yun. Sin can imagine that lives for his sister and their father must be very hard during the Japanese occupation of Hong Kong.

Without too many options, Sin's mother and her two sons walked from Macao to their home village Yanbu (鹽步), which is now amalgamated into today's Nanhai District (which is part of Foshan Prefecture), in the Guangdong Province of China. The distance between Macao and Nanhai is about 110 kilometres. According to Keung, he carried Foo on his back with a *mei tai* (咩帶) during the foot journey back to China. Keung was nine years old at that time, and Foo was only three years old and was too young at that time to remember this. Due to the lack of vitamin A in his diet, Foo temporary suffered night blindness while the family was living in Macao. His condition was detected and cured by taking foods rich in vitamin-A.

In the autumn of 1943, the family decided to reunite again. Keung and Foo journeyed back to Hong Kong by land and by sea with their mother, their father anxiously awaited for their arrival on Nam Cheong Street[1] of Sham Shui Po. At that time Foo was a little older, and towards the end of the War, he remembers the aerial bombings by the allied forces in his neighbourhood of Sham Shui Po. During the year that the War ended, the family lived for a short period on Ki Lung Street before they moved to Pei Ho Street.

Sin's father, whose name was Wah (華), was born in the first decade of the twentieth century in China. Wah married Pang Kwai (彭葵) in his hometown, and had daughter Yun and son Keung before immigrating to Hong Kong in the 1930s. Foo was the second son born in Hong Kong in 1938.

Wah's upbringing was from the old style of schooling in China around the second and third decades of the 20th century, with Confucian classics formed the core of learning, and maybe augmented by some western technology teachings. Without any skill training, it was difficult for him to seek suitable employment in Hong Kong during the pre- and post-WWII period. But Wah was very innovative and was not afraid to take chances in business. The reason he came to Hong Kong as a young man was to seek good business breaks. As mentioned in Chapter 2, Sin's great grandfather had a daughter and four sons. It was the great grandfather's youngest son (Wah's uncle) who went to Hong Kong and established for himself a small factory to produce soap and a retail shop to sell soap and other household items. So, taking some leads from his uncle in Hong Kong, Wah was able to venture into business.

Wah was an entrepreneur before, during and after the War. Before the War, he had started a small business selling items as a street hawker, and during the War he made home-made Soya sauce and sold them in a store on Pei Ho Street. After the War, he made and sold wax papers, wooden matches, and started a number of other home base projects in 171 Pei Ho Street. But due to lack of business training and luck, he did not get ahead with any of these business endeavours.

After the War ended, the family was poor-stricken and was struggling to recover from poverty. For about twenty-three years of his life in Hong Kong, Wah was either self-employed, taking temporary employment, or unemployed. Ten years after the War, the hardship of life and disappointment had caused Wah to have emotional anxiety that eventually made him ill mentally; it weakened his body's ability to ward off the commutable tuberculosis. In the fall of 1955, Wah was admitted to a mental institution in Hong Kong and in the summer of the following year, he passed away in that institution. He was forty-eight years old.

A renovated *tong lau* at 119-121 Nam Cheong Street

CHAPTER FOUR

Memories of his Parents

S in has fond memories of his father. Wah died when Sin was only eight years old. Sin remembers his father had a kind fatherly look; he had a thin face, covered by a 2-3 days old beard, and had a head of grey hair. He only wore the Chinese traditional pajamas or kung fu suits and kung fu shoes for nearly all occasions. The family used to have a portrait of him posing in this attire and wearing a fedora, but after Wah passed away, Sin's mother did not want to be reminded of his death and she removed the picture from the living room.

Wah started to teach Sin to practice Chinese calligraphy at home with an ink brush, and taught Sin how to read and write Chinese before he formally attended his Primary 1 class at school. Sin has recollections of the celebration of the coronation of Queen Elizabeth

II, and vaguely remembers that his father took him to a balcony of a house where he could look down and watch the parades on the streets of Kowloon. Sin's father used to take him to a local restaurant, the Pei Ho Restaurant, to *"yum cha"* (飲茶) and for eating dim sum in the morning. *Yum cha*, in Cantonese literally means "drink tea"; it is a Chinese style morning or afternoon tea which involves tasting Chinese tea and eating dim sum dishes.

Sin remembers his mother as a petit woman with straight neck-length hair combing back from the forehead, and she used two hair clips, one on each side of the head, to hold the hair behind the ears. Her usual wardrobes were lady style Chinese traditional pyjamas, but on occasions such as dinner functions, she would wear the *cheongsam* (長衫). Being the youngest child of the family, Sin had the advantage of receiving undivided love and attention from his mother.

When he was very young and got sick with the flu or some other aliment, his mother would take him to the Sham Shui Po Public Dispensary[2] on Yee Kuk Street, near the old Sham Shui Po Ferry Pier. The Dispensary was a walk-in clinic that provided free medical attention and dispensary drugs for the grassroot population of Sham Shui Po. The only negative side of this clinic was that it operated on a first-come-first-serve system and a daily quota, so patients had to wait in a queue outside the clinic early in the morning before the clinic's opening hours if they wanted to see the doctor-on-duty. Sometimes, Sin's mother would take him to a traditional Chinese medicine practitioner but Sin preferred the Public Dispensary. The traditional Chinese herbal medicine practitioner, Mr. Cho (曹懵塵醫師), diagnosed his patients in his herbal shop located on Cheung Sha Wan Road. The waiting time in this herbal shop was not as long as the Public Dispensary, because Mr. Cho attended his patients quite quickly by pulse palpation using traditional Chinese medicine diagnostic technique. At the end of the diagnosis Mr. Cho would prescribe a cocktail of herbs for Sin to make the tea as remedy specifically for the illness. Sin did not like the bitter taste of the prescribed herbal tea he had to take, but nonetheless, it did have the curing effects for common colds and flu.

After the death of Sin's father, his mother embraced Taoism as a religion, and as a Taoist she abstained from eating beef. On the fifteenth day of the seventh month in the lunar calendar (the day is called Ghost Day in Chinese tradition), his mother would go to the Taoist temple to give offerings to the deceased ancestors by burning Joss paper, and to request the deceased ancestors to bestow their blessings upon the living descendants. She really believed that her husband would help their sons to be successful one day.

137 Yee Kuk Street Sham Shui Po Public Dispensary

CHAPTER FIVE

Remembering the Deceased Relatives

W ah's younger brother Kwan (坤) and elder sister were also living in Hong Kong during the War. Wah's elder sister was married to Mr. Ngan Gen Ha (顏鏡夏), who worked as an inspector for the Health Department in Hong Kong. In the 1960s, she immigrated to Canada with her family. Sin visited his aunt in Vancouver in 1987 and that was the last time a member of the Fung family contacted her before she passed away.

After the War, Uncle Kwan (坤) was working in a small printing shop. His employment was not very steady, and therefore after Sin's father had passed away, Uncle Kwan managed to spend quite some time with Sin by taking him around, and sometimes taking him to his print shop. Even at his young age, Sin knew how difficult life was for the unemployed, because Uncle Kwan was so tight in money that occasionally, he had to borrow from Sin's piggy bank (money that Sin received from red envelope or *lai see* 利是, during the Chinese New Year). Sin gladly obliged to please his uncle, because with the money, Uncle Kwan would take Sin to a restaurant for a nice meal. Uncle Kwan's first wife died during the War, and he re-married again in the 1960s. In 1977, Uncle Kwan was hired by Keung to work in his factory's warehouse in Kwai Chung.

Uncle Kwan and his wife died childless, Keung and Foo took care of their burials and their remains were placed in a wall niche in a memorial garden in the New Territories, Kowloon.

Sin remembers the name of his grandmother from his mother's side. Her name was Chan Mua Ching (陳茂清). Sin's mother took Sin to Macao ones to visit his grandmother in the early 1950s. She was living in the Island of Taipa in Macao, and the main industry in Taipa at that time was firecrackers. She lived on and off in Hong Kong with Sin's family during the 1950s, but during the War, Grandma Chan lived in Taipa. While she was staying in Hong Kong, she often asked Sin to write letters for her because she was illiterate, and that's why he could remember her name. Grandma Chan died in the late 1960s.

CHAPTER SIX

Sin's Early Schooling Years

Sin attended his first primary school on Kweilin Street in the Sham Shui Po district of west Kowloon. This school was a privately-ran neighbourhood school. In the early 1950s, government-ran public primary schools were scarce and admission was difficult. Therefore, kids who could not go to public schools would have to go to the affordable neighbourhood schools ran by private operators. Kindergarten classes were not included in the public school system; Sin's parents did not send him to private kindergarten classes because in those days, it was considered just for the kids of rich families to attend.

Sin has vivid memories of the first primary school he started to attend in 1954. It was a Chinese school and its curriculum was very basic. This school was located in a *tong lau* (唐樓) building which was converted into a privately-ran neighbourhood school. The desks and chairs in the classrooms were roughly finished and the blackboards in some classrooms were not centred but off to one side at the front. The classrooms were very small and lighting was barely sufficient in the morning during the winter months. The school was owned and operated by the headmaster who ran the school like a business and had over-crowded classrooms illegally. Sin remembers that on some occasions, his classroom teacher had to take some students to hide in the washroom when the education department inspector was around to check the school.

Suggested by Keung to switch to an English primary school in 1956, Sin started to attend this new school quite a distance away from home. Sin learned to be very independent at a very young age. For three years, he had to take a long bus ride from Sham Shui Po to Ngau Chi Wan every day to attend this school. Sham Shui Po is in West Kowloon and Ngau Chi Wan is in East Kowloon. Small kids nowadays in Hong Kong can take private school buses to their schools and are well taken care of by a 'bus mother' on the bus. Maybe the world was quite different in the 1950s, because Sin remembers that he had a couple of schoolmates living in the same area who also travelled daily on the same bus route to attend the same school. It seemed that Sin's mother was less concerned about the safety of Sin's daily bus ride, or maybe at that time she had no alternatives but to secure her job in the daytime, and Sin had to take care of his own daily chores. For breakfast, Sin simply went down the street to a *dai pai dong* (大排檔) to buy himself something to eat; a bowl of rice porridge or congee, a fried bread stick (*yau tiu,* 油條), or steamed rice rolls (*cheung fun,* 腸粉). Later in the morning, Sin would cook and eat his lunch at home before going to take the bus ride to his half-day school at Ngau Chi Wan.

This new school that Sin attended was the Good Hope Primary School. Today the Good Hope School in Hong Kong is an all girls school with primary and secondary sections, but back in 1956, the primary section accepted boys and girls students. Attending this school really helped Sin to develop his foundation of the English language; the school used English only to teach all subjects, with the exception of the Chinese language which was a compulsory subject. Sin was happy to attend this school and adapted to the system very quickly.

This school in comparison to the one in Sham Shui Po was like day and night. It had proper desks and chairs for the students, all of the classrooms had windows and were bright and well-lit. The school had a tuck shop for students to buy drinks and snacks, and a school gym for daily gathering prior to class commencements. There was an outdoor basketball court with a lot of open space surrounding the school property because it was located on a hill in the outskirt of Ngau Chi Wan, an area that was very under-developed during the mid-1950s. The school overlooked a stone quarry mine that was located at a lower elevation and quite a distant away. Everyday at noon and at five in the afternoon, the mine would generate a minute of 'gong' warning sound, and then blasting sounds of controlled explosions could be heard. To get to the school from the Ngau Chi Wan bus stop, students had to take the school shuttle bus that ran uphill on the old Clear Water Bay Road. This stretch of road entwined downhill from the school passing through small patches of farmlands, and the old Dairy Farm cowsheds along one side of the road, before reaching the Ngau Chi Wan bus stop. Sometimes after school, Sin and his classmates would walk downhill on the old Clear Water Bay Road instead of taking the shuttle bus. As school kids, walking down that road was considered fun and an adventure, they didn't worry about safety while walking on a road that did not have sidewalks for pedestrians.

The Good Hope Primary School was a Catholic school, but Sin's first exposure to the Catholic religion was not from this school. When Foo was a teenager, he took Sin to the St. Francis of Assisi Catholic Church[3] on Shek Kip Mei Street to receive occasional handouts given to the local residents of Sham Shui Po, such as bags of white rice or corn flour, and sometimes packages of imported cheese. Also, an old lady tenant (she was called by everyone as *Ma Po*, 馬婆) at 171 Pei Ho Street (more details about 171 Pei Ho Street in Chapter 7) took Sin to this church to listen to the evening gospel preaching class for a period of time around 1956-1957.

Although Keung was busy with his business, he took interest in Sin's schooling and guided him to choose the proper school to attend. In the spring of 1959, Keung told Sin to try to apply for the fall semester as a new student of the La Salle Primary School. At the time, Sin was just a young child and did not know much about the school system in Hong Kong. The La Salle Primary School had a major expansion in that year, and she was going to accept additional students, therefore the school had a set date for applicants to write an admission examination. It turned out that Sin was lucky enough to pass the admission examination and was accepted by the La Salle Primary School. And so in September of 1959, Sin began to attend the La Salle Primary School. This change had even more of a profound effect on Sin's education. La Salle Primary School and La Salle College are government Grant Schools. Students graduated from the primary school were automatically promoted to the secondary school, the La Salle College. This school is quite famous in Hong Kong for the quality of teaching, and the academic and athletic standings among the secondary schools of the city. English is the primary language used for teaching in the La Salle Primary School and La Salle College.

Shek Kip Mei Street St. Francis of Assisi Catholic Church

CHAPTER SEVEN

171 Pei Ho Street in Kowloon

Sin was born in Sham Shui Po, and for the first eleven years of his childhood, he lived in 171 Pei Ho Street[4]. This address held significance to the entire family; it provided a stable and permanent address for the family after the War from 1946 to 1959. It was not only where all the brothers grew up, Yun raised her family in this home for a period of time, and it was also the start-up location of Keung's plastic artificial flowers business.

Sin estimates that the building was originally built in the pre-WWII timeframe. The building was built in continuous blocks with long narrow units on Pei Ho Street; Sin's family lived in the unit number 171 which was an end unit. It was a multi-family dwelling building, a balcony-type tenement building called *tong lau* (唐樓), which was designed for both residential and commercial uses. The upper floors of *tong lau* buildings were for residential use and occupied by Chinese residents. The ground floor portion could be reserved for commercial use, such as a local store similar to today's mini-supermarket or convenient grocery shop, a machine shop, or a restaurant. Similar *tong laus* could be found in other streets neighbouring Pei Ho Street. Sin remembers that Nam Cheong Street[5] had a number of shops that produced hand-made copper and brass basins and vases.

The building where Sin lived had three storeys above the ground floor. The *tong lau* unit had a narrow straight-flight of walled staircase that started from street level, and the adjacent row unit was separated by the left wall of the staircase. There was a landing halfway up the staircase with a door located sideways on the right wall for entering to the second floor; continuing straight up the staircase was the entrance door of the third floor. Entering into the third floor from this entrance door was a vestibule. One end of the vestibule linked to a small passage way leading to a small storage room, the bathroom, and then to the kitchen room, all located at the rear of the flat. To the right of the vestibule was an open walkway that circumvented the storage room and the bathroom, and provided an alternative entry point to the kitchen room. The walkway had a waist-high railing; the rear section of the flats was only half of the unit's lot width, therefore residents standing on this walkway could talk to other residents that happened to be on the walkway on the floor above or below, they also could look down onto an open court on the ground floor below. When he was a young boy, Sin liked to throw paper airplanes from this walkway and watched how far they could fly.

On the third floor there was another straight-flight of staircase at the other end of the vestibule for going up to the rear section of the fourth floor. Tenants living on the fourth floor had to enter into the third floor first and then proceed upwards by using this flight of stairs.

The fourth floor had a smaller living area than the third floor below, the facade of the fourth floor recessed to form an open balcony of a few feet extended beyond the front. The roof of the unit could only be accessed from the fourth floor. When Sin was a small kid, Foo sometimes took him to the roof on summer days to fly a kite there; they were quite acquainted with couple of young boys living on the fourth floor.

The old Pei Ho Street had characteristics of a grass root community in that era. It was a busy street that lined with mostly pre-war *tong lau* buildings on both sides. Pei Ho Street was a busy street for two reasons. Firstly, the west end of the street was waterfront, there stood a pier for the Yaumatei Ferry (now defunct) to provide services to and from Central and Sheung Wan on the Hong Kong side, therefore there was a constant flow of ferry passengers along the west end of the street. Secondly, further up from the pier, the western section of the street was like a market place. There was a market building on one side of the street and street hawkers positioned themselves in the middle of the pavement; they sold food and fresh produce to compete with the licensed vendors inside the market building. The east end of the street ended at the Mark 1 Resettlement Estates of Shek Kip Mei. 171 Pei Ho Street is near the east end of the street.

There were two cinemas on the street for showing Hong-Kong-produced movies, Sin's mother preferred the Pei Ho Theatre because she liked to watch movies featuring famous Cantonese opera singers. Cartoons from Hollywood were shown on Sunday mornings at this theatre, and for movie goers who liked foreign film, different re-run western movies were on the 5:30 p.m. showtime daily. Admission for the 5:30 p.m. show was less than the regular now-playing movies. Street hawkers would gather in front of the theatre selling ready-to-eat food to cinema-goers. The variety of food that was sold included: roasted chestnuts, *lo shui* (Cantonese, 滷水) marinated cold cuts (such as beef, pork liver, chicken giblets, and chicken feet), fresh fruits, pickled vegetables, and many other tasty treats. Inside the theatre before the show began, some independent vendors with the approval from the theatre sold ice-cream bars and candies to the patrons in their seats.

The Sham Shui Po district that Sin was familiar with was an area of residential mixed with factories for light manufacturing. Textile and garment workers could live on one street and go to work in a factory on the next street within walking distance. In those days, a garment manufacturer could be located in a residential building that was used as a factory to suit the needs. Working conditions such as lighting, air circulation and conditioning, and noise elimination and control were usually very poor. Most workers could be working and having lunch breaks in the same workstations. No matter what the conditions were, the workers in those days strived and made a living to raise their families, but most importantly they were the nameless builders of Hong Kong today. Although Sham Shui Po is a low income district in Hong Kong, it is not necessary that the people who live there will remain poor. Keung is from Sham Shui Po and is a self-made millionaire. Today, Sham Shui Po has passed its era of providing manufacturing jobs to its residence, it has transformed into a hotspot for shopping for electronics and accessories, fashion wears and fabrics.

Sin's family moved into the third floor of 171 Pei Ho Street as the original tenant in 1946. The total living area of the flat was about 700 square feet, including the balcony. The facade of the third floor recessed to form an open balcony of about eight feet extended beyond the front living area, with French style wood and glass doors separating the front living area and the balcony. Sin remembers that when he was

start-up business. In 1958 the entire balcony had another makeover. The machine shop was moved to a factory location, and walls were erected on three sides of the balcony, converting it into a bedroom and a living room. The reason for constructing this additional space was because Keung was getting married and this new bedroom would be occupied by him and his bride. In the summer of 1958 Keung got married. He and his new bride, Shum Won To (岑旺桃), lived in 171 Pei Ho Street during the first year of their married lives. After all the adversities that happened to the family in the mid-1950s, it was elated again with a wedding in August of 1958. The family had a wedding reception at a Chinese restaurant on Shanghai Street, Kowloon, and invited all the relatives and friends of the Fung family. The family was excited when they found out in October that Keung's wife was pregnant and expected to give birth next year.

Sin's family moved out of 171 Pei Ho Street in 1959 and his sister's family moved into this same address the following year, but later, the *tong lau* was acquired by developers for redevelopment, and Yun's family had to move out from there.

Today, more than half a century later, the poor residents in Sham Shui Po district still have to endure crowded living conditions. It will cost over HK$2,000 for a family to rent a cubicle-style unit (of about 60 square feet) with proper walls, doors and a private bathroom in a sub-divided flat. The family might have to do the cooking in the bathroom area, and sit around a two-square-feet table beside the bunker bed to eat their dinners. This family may gain a little more privacy than their counterparts in the 1950s, but they have to pay more than 200 times in rent! In 2011, while Sin was visiting Hong Kong, he went back to the neighbourhood of Pei Ho Street to take a look. The *tong lau* block where 171 Pei Ho Street stood was torn down for some years ago and now a new building is standing at that location.

A *tong lau* at 181-183 Pei Ho Street

Street scene at 117-125 Nam Cheong Street

CHAPTER EIGHT

Sin was Taken Care of by
His Siblings

S in's family was quite down-and-out in the early 1950s
because Sin's father was unemployed for a number of years
after the War. 1955 was a bad year for the family because
Sin's father became ill and eventually died in 1956. Keung's second
start-up business was not successful and he had to seek employment
with a plastic manufacturing company. Foo terminated his Form 3
(equivalent to Grade 9) education after the death of his father to take
an apprenticeship at a local machine shop on Tai Nan Street in Sham
Shui Po, simply because there was not enough money in the family
for him to continue his schooling. Sin's mother began working in a
factory on Fuk Wing Street as a garment worker to support Sin to go

to school. Sin was pretty much all alone by himself at that time, trying to cope with the death of his father.

Sin's life was not in turmoil, nor was it ordinary for a boy of his age. Despite losing a parent at his young age, Sin was a happy, responsible and independent kid. Living in 171 Pei Ho Street had trained Sin to be tolerant with his fellow residents on the same flat, to be flexible and contented with the living standard that was available to him. He did not have the luxury of having a bedroom, most of the time in the evening he put his bed either in the balcony, or in the vestibule area beside the stairway for the fourth floor. His bed was either an army cot bed or just a makeshift one consisted of three long wood planks supported by two narrow wooden benches at both ends. Sometimes he slept on the elevated wooden mezzanine above the storage room at the back end of the flat. There was no heating in the building, so it was quite cold on some winter nights.

Despite of the living conditions Sin considered himself luckier than the other kids on the same flat at 171 Pei Ho Street; in 1956 he attended a decent school for his education while the other kids did not have the same opportunity. Comparing his childhood life with his three siblings, Sin considered him more fortunate because his siblings had to endure worse living conditions, hunger, disruptive schooling, and temporary family separation, all because of the War.

Sin received care and support from his siblings, especially from Yun. Two years after the War, Yun married Mui Lit (梅烈) in Jiujiang, Guangdong, China. According to Keung, he told Sin that Yun's marriage was arranged by their father. In 1949, Yun and her husband decided to migrate back to Hong Kong to stay close with her parents.

Yun started to have a family of her own. In those days, most households that were not financially secured would require both parents to work to support the families. To help the family income and to look after her children, Yun worked as a stay-at-home seamstress by taking the pre-cut garment fabrics from a nearby garment factory and did the sewing at home, using a manual Singer sewing machine. When Sin was a young boy, he enjoyed visiting his sister and staying over for a week or so during the summer holidays, and playing with his nephews who were all younger than him. She was like a second caregiver to Sin when his mother was not around, and she had a tendency to spoil Sin in front of her own children.

Despite having four children of her own at that time, after their father had passed away Yun took care of Sin as much as she could. She welcomed him to her home for dinner after school in the evening because Sin's mother was working late in the garment factory. At that time, Yun's family rented a partitioned room in a *tong lau,* not too far away from Pei Ho Street. In 1957, Yun's family moved to Whitty Street, in the Shek Tong Tsui district of the Hong Kong Island, and lived there until 1960, and then they moved to 171 Pei Ho Street.

Sin has happy memories of growing up as a child with Foo. It was Foo who taught Sin at a very young age to play the harmonica and took Sin to swim at the Lai Chi Kok Beach. Foo also took his kid brother to the Lai Chi Kok Amusement Park which was where Sin had the most fun, or to the theatres on Nathan Road for western movies. These two siblings were much closer because of the least difference in age between them. As for Keung, he was the pillar of the family after the death of their father and had a special place in his heart for Sin. Keung always ensured Sin received a good education to better his future, and he was there to make sure that Sin attended the proper school. When Sin began to attend the Good Hope School, Keung spent time in the evening with his young brother to make sure that he could catch up with his homework from the new school.

But during his adolescent years, Sin began to drift apart from his two brothers, due to the large age differences and their busy work lives, he made less of an attempt to communicate much with them. Now looking back, Sin wishes that he had spent more time with them and had built a closer relationship with his brothers.

CHAPTER NINE

Keung is An Entrepreneur

Yun once told Sin that their grandfather was a man with mechanical aptitudes. According to Yun's story, their grandfather was very keen on the rice huller or rice husker machines in those days, and he could pinpoint a mechanical problem by just listening to the noise that the machine was making. Although this story could not be verified now, Keung has traits of intelligence related to mechanical and machinery equipment. Yun told Sin another story that took place during WWII; while Keung was a young boy and living in Macao, he made use of some scrap sheet metal to make whistles and then sold them as toys. As a kid Keung also liked to take a mechanical item apart and then reassembled it back together again.

Keung was born in 1933 in Yanbu (鹽步) on the 19th day of the 2nd lunar month, which is the birthday of *Kuan Yin* (觀音), and *Kuan Yin* is the Chinese name for Avalokiteśvara. Chinese believe that people born on the birthday of *Kuan Yin* would receive lifetime blessings and luck from the bodhisattva (菩薩).

Keung's hometown, Yanbu, is amalgamated into today's Nanhai District (which is in Foshan Prefecture), Guangdong Province, China. Although the village of Yanbu does not formally exist now, a few local businesses located in Nanhai are still having their company names containing the words Yanbu (鹽步) to indicate their roots.

Keung's earliest childhood memory was when he was about two years of age; his father took him to Queen's Road West in Sai Wan, Hong Kong to watch the welcoming parade for the official visit of Prince Albert, the Duke of York (who became King George VI).

In 1947, Keung took an apprentice job in a local machine shop on Fuk Wing Street in Sham Shui Po and was paid a salary of ten Hong Kong dollars per month. This was necessary for Keung because the family was poor and there was not enough money for him to continue his education that charged eighty Hong Kong dollars per semester in those days.

In the first few years after the War in Hong Kong, being an apprentice of any trade was not an easy job. In the machine shop he was the lowest on the totem pole and had to do all the chores, including buying fresh meat and produce from the Sham Shui Po market on Pei Ho Street, and cooking the daily meals for the staff members of the shop. In old Hong Kong, it was common for an owner/boss of a small family-type business (such as a food store, retail store, or a machine shop) to provide two meals daily to the staff, right in the store or shop. Most stores or shops in the area of Sham Shui Po were ground floor units of the *tong lau* blocks, and each unit had a kitchen at the back of the premise.

Keung slept on an army cot bed at the machine shop at night because he was responsible for cleaning and closing the shop nightly. During the day, Keung would learn about the trade by following the boss or a staff member who was more senior and knowledgeable and acted as mentor. Such apprenticeship was not a formal training program sponsored by the education department, 'graduating' at the end of the apprenticeship would not earn any official recognition. In those days, it was sufficient for young people who did not have higher or formal education to learn a trade or skill for career development.

After two or three years of apprenticeship, Keung 'graduated' from his training at the machine shop and was very eager to start a business of his own. In the early 1950s, Hong Kong was impoverished by the War and to rebuild the society she needed all kinds of manufactured goods and accessories. Keung's business idea was to make injection moulds to produce plastic buttons for garments in addition to the normal business of a machine shop. He started to make injection moulds for plastic buttons at the 171 Pei Ho Street location. In 1951, he set up his shop on Un Chau Street in Sham Shui Po, later in 1953 his shop was moved to an area called To Kwa Wan, which was an industrial area in Kowloon at that time. His main customer was a nearby plastic manufacturing company that produced toys, and Keung's shop was to produce the injection moulds for this plastic manufacturing company. However, in 1954 this plastic manufacturer temporary stopped its operation due to moving to another factory location. The sale of the plastic buttons was not performing well enough to sustain the shop's operating costs, and it was tough to do business with the local garment industry if one did not have the right connections. In addition to bad timing, decreased work orders, and economic woes forced Keung to sell his machinery and wound-up the business.

The next year, Keung and Mr. Chi Hing Chan, a friend of Keung's father, started a home-base toy project on Lockhart Road, Wan Chai. With a limited amount of seed money, they invested in a horizontal injection molding machine. Keung was working at this location without a salary, and instead, he would just receive two daily meals from Mr. Chan's household. Keung's daily routine was to take the ferry from the Sham Shui Po pier to Wan Chai, worked at Lockhart Road until the end of the day, and then took the ferry back to Sham Shui Po, Pei Ho Street. In this home-base project, Keung designed and produced a pull-string flywheel toy. The flywheel was made out of plastic, and it could make a whistling sound while spinning. The spin was initiated manually by holding both ends of the pull-string and twirling the flywheel to start the rotation around its own central axis. By tightening and loosening the tension of the pull-string, the spinning motion could be sustained. Unfortunately this business endeavor was not successful within the first year to obtain a sizable order; Mr. C.H. Chan decided to end the 'basement' project.

After the Lockhart Road project, Keung was approached by the owner of the same plastic manufacturing company at To Kwa Wan and was offered a supervisor position in the machine shop department at the company's new location. Keung's base salary was HK$200 per month and he was in charge of producing plastic injection moulds; he also received a 5% bonus on every mould produced for other customers. So Keung was an employee from 1956 to 1957, and it was quite a tranquil period for him after two disappointing failures at his business attempts. Sin remembers sharing the balcony shed with Keung on the flat of 171 Pei Ho Street. When his brother came home from work, Keung would spend his evening hours reading the very popular Chinese kungfu novels by Jin Yong (金庸), and sharing a bottle of San Miguel brew with Sin. Yes, Sin was drinking under-age but big brother did not intend to poison his young brother, and one small glass of beer could not do much harm on a hot summer night!

It was 1957 and after working about two years as an employee, Keung did not give up his entrepreneurial dreams and decided to launch a comeback. Because he was keen on making injection moulds and saw the rising trend of using plastic artificial flowers for household and commercial decorations, Keung decided to take this business opportunity to produce plastic artificial flowers. His initial plan was to set up a pilot project at 171 Pei Ho Street. His first step involved converting the balcony of 171 Pei Ho Street into a makeshift machine room which he had equipped with a lathe machine, a drill press, a milling machine, a heavy-duty wooden work bench, bench vices, various mechanical tools, and the horizontal injection molding machine which Keung had retrieved from the Lockhart Road project.

At the age of 25, Keung's determination to have a business of his own became a reality. With the help of Foo and a couple of friends, the second step was to start producing the proto-type moulds for some simple foliage-contour leaves and flower petals. After the moulds were made, they were used to produce the plastic leaves and flower petals by using the injection molding machine. With perseverance and patience, and a long trial and error process, Keung's team fine tuned the moulds. They mastered the right thickness of the leaves and flower petals, used the proper mix of industrial colour dye powders and the plastic granules to produce the right colour tones for the proto-type products.

Things were starting to turn around for Keung in 1958. His project began to be on track and finally came to fruition. The sleepless nights of working around the clock experimenting and trial testing finally paid off. Keung co-operated with a business partner, Mr. P.M. Leung, and through him, they managed to obtain purchase orders for plastic artificial flowers from a local export firm. Towards the summer of 1958, his makeshift workshop was moved from 171 Pei Ho Street to his first factory located in an industrial unit on Larch Street in Tai Kok Tsui, Kowloon. By that time, Foo was already a formal employee of his brother. The factory also hired a number of women workers to assemble the plastic floral parts and leaves into finished stem flowers. His first taste of success was earned by not just from luck or blessings from *Kwan Yin*. Keung had to strive during the first year's operation of the factory in order to bring it on track. He put all his efforts into the business, especially when meeting deadlines for delivery of the products, he had to stay in the factory around the clock to manage the production.

CHAPTER TEN

Hong Kong Was Waking Up in the 1960s

The family's fortune was stepping in the right direction in 1959. Keung's factory was making profits after one year of operation. Keung's mother no longer had to go to work in the factory because Keung was able to support the family comfortably. At that time, Foo was employed by his brother and worked in the factory's machine shop department that produced the moulds for the various floral components. In June of that year, Keung's wife Shum Won To[6] (岑旺桃) gave birth to a baby girl and her name was Wai Yu[7] (慧茹). In September of 1959, the family moved out of Sham Shui Po, into a unit within an apartment complex located in a better

43

neighbourhood of Kowloon, on Prince Edward Road. Keung bought his first car, a Hillman Saloon, in 1959.

The move was exceptionally happy for Sin because the new home was much closer for him to go to the La Salle Primary School, which Sin had started to attend beginning in September of 1959. For the first time in Sin's life, he could enjoy the bathroom vanities of using a bathtub to bathe, and using a toilet in the comfort of his own home. This was heaven in comparison to 171 Pei Ho Street.

In the 1950s, the old Prince Edward Road ran from west to east, starting from Tai Kok Tsui, and eastward to Mong Kok, Kowloon Tong and Kowloon City. The road section between Kowloon Tong and Kowloon City was wide and beautiful; it ran through a nice neighbourhood with mostly single detached villa-style houses on both sides. Beyond Kowloon City, the east extension of the old Prince Edward Road changed its name before terminating into Ngau Chi Wan. Sin was familiar with the old Prince Edward Road because, for three years, he rode daily on the Kowloon Motor Bus route 2A that ran on this road to Ngau Chi Wan for attending the Good Hope Primary School. Sin would not have dreamt that his new home in 1959 would be on the Prince Edward Road. Sin was very familiar with the stretch of the Prince Edward Road from the Embankment Road going east to La Salle Road. He walked on this stretch of road daily to his primary school, and then the secondary school, from 1959 to 1968.

Sin noticed the changes that took place on both sides of the road. The villa-style detached houses, most of them with front iron-rod gates and front gardens, were slowly purchased by developers and were demolished and replaced by high rise apartment buildings. The new buildings were initially built with modest basic designs, but towards the late 1960s, the newer ones were luxurious and had up-to-date

.tectural style and design features. The construction business was revamped with new detailed guidelines for the first time since WWII. This was much needed progress, the real estate market boom in that neighbourhood was about to begin due to the demand from the growing middle and upper middle income classes. There are a number of so-called 'famous schools' in this particular area of Kowloon, and this is the reason that the increased demand and value for real estate is still evident today.

The 1960s were probably the decade in defining the identity of Hong Kong as it is today. Hong Kong experienced a new decade of industrial growth in the manufacturing sector. The textile industry used to be the foundation of boosting the economy, but in the sixties, manufacturing for various light industries were growing at a fast pace. In 1962, Keung's plastic flower factory moved to an industrial unit at the Wah Yuen Factory Building (located on Beech Street in Tai Kok Tsui), with production floor space expanded to more than five thousand square feet. This was a major milestone because the factory now had its premises that were owned by the business. In 1966, Keung started a toy factory with business partners Mr. P.M. Leung and Mr. W.K. Tung. This was not only a business decision, but a personal one for Keung because he enjoyed the challenges of using his mechanical intellect in the designing of toys.

In 1962, Sin had completed his primary school and began his secondary school education at the La Salle College. Keung's family had grown by the additions of four children of his own; therefore it was once again moving time. Being the oldest son of the family, Keung took on the responsibility as the head of a traditional Chinese family after their father had passed away. In a traditional Chinese family, parents and unwed children could live in the same household; therefore the apartment unit on Prince Edward Road was a bit too small for them. In the same year, the family moved to a new and bigger apartment in Mong Kok. This apartment was located on the Playing Field Road, which was near the intersection of Prince Edward Road and Nathan Road. The family had their first television set in this apartment.

There were several major events that happened in Hong Kong at that time. In 1962, Typhoon Wanda hit Hong Kong and caused 183 casualties. Hong Kong's fresh water supply depended on rain water gathered in man-made reservoirs, and in 1963, after a prolonged draught period, water supply was rationed to four hours a day. The 1966 riots, or often called as the Star Ferry riots, were caused by social dissatisfaction over the increase in fares by the Star Ferry Company. At that time before the Cross-Harbour Tunnel was built, the Star Ferry was mainly relied on by commuters to cross the harbour between Tsim Sha Tsui, Kowloon and Hong Kong Island's Central district. The riot in 1967 that was triggered by a labour dispute in an artificial flower factory in San Po Kong, was really the reflections of the Chinese Cultural Revolution in mainland China.

In 1960s, the people of Hong Kong enjoyed the growing prosperity and progress made in that era, but also paid for the price caused by man-made or natural disasters. Life went on with the Fung family. Keung had four school-age daughters (慧茹, 慧茵, 慧嫻, 慧瓊) in his family, and Keung's mother had a fair share of work looking after the granddaughters. Yun had a bigger family of her own; she had seven school-age children. While Foo was gainfully employed by Keung, Sin had just written the Hong Kong English School Certificate Examination in 1967, a year that was marked with social unrest and riot in Hong Kong. In 1968, Sin was trying to figure out his continuing education and with the financial support from his brother, he chose to go abroad to Canada for his post-secondary school education.

Photo of Foo, Keung, Shum Won To and daughter

Photo of Sin and Wai Yu

CHAPTER ELEVEN

The Turning Points of the Lives of the Siblings

S in did not realize the importance and influential role Keung had not only in his life but his siblings until this latest visit to Hong Kong in 2012. During the family gathering dinner, it dawned on Sin that Keung was an unimposing person, and yet everything he did for his siblings were acts of brotherly love.

Ever since the death of his father, Sin looked upon Keung as his guardian and provider of guidance. 1956 was the turning point for Sin. After the loss of his father, Sin received guidance from his brother that he should choose to attend an English school. This was perhaps the most important step for Sin in his early education. Attending the Good Hope Primary School provided Sin the proficiency in

English that enabled him to later attend the famous La Salle Primary School and the La Salle College in Hong Kong. After he completed his secondary school education, Sin left Hong Kong for Canada to further his study in electrical engineering, with the financial support from Keung. Sin felt very much indebted to his brother's generosity and support he had received in his childhood and early adult years. Sin's sister once told him that Keung was hoping that Sin would come back to Hong Kong after graduation to take a job at his factory. However Sin had other plans of his own. After Sin graduated in 1973, he decided to stay in Canada to work as an engineer, and a year later, he married Karen.

Foo became an employee of Keung from 1958 to 1968, but from 1969 to 1977, he and some of his co-workers started another plastic factory, and then in 1977, he rejoined his brother again as a minority shareholder. Keung's trusted employee and business partner was his brother Foo, who had gone through all the ups and downs with Keung's plastic artificial flower factory, and then later, the toy factory. If Sin had to pick the turning point in Foo's life, it would be the year of 1942. The song *"He Ain't Heavy, He's My Brother"* by the Hollies would play in Sin's mind whenever he pictured Keung carrying Foo on his back during their foot journey from Macao to China. Sin's eyes would weld up with emotion at that thought of love and sacrifice. It turned out that Foo's career path was very similar to Keung's, both of them started as an apprentice in a machine shop. But later in life, Foo received more than a helping hand from his elder brother, who became successful in his business and provided Foo with a job initially, and then a partnership deal in 1977. Keung's initial business partner, Mr. P.M. Leung, often complained to Keung that his younger brother Foo was setting up a side business of his own to compete with them. This was an accusation without any base, and Keung stood by his brother and defended him. Mr. P.M. Leung immigrated to the U.S. and broke off the business partnership with Keung in 1967.

Foo got married in the early 1970s, and started to have a family of his own. By 1973 he had a son and a daughter; Foo's mother chose to stay with her second son to take care of the young grand children. At that time, Foo's family and his mother stayed in the apartment on Playing Field Road, while Keung's family had already moved out and into another apartment located on the 'famous schools' section of Prince Edward Road. The last time Sin saw his mother was in the summer of 1974, the year that he got married and went back to Hong Kong with Karen for their honeymoon. In the spring of 1975, Sin's mother passed away due to lung cancer. She was 63.

Having seven children of her own, Yun and her husband were working very hard to maintain a household of nine. To ameliorate their condition, Keung helped his sister in a very subtle way. In the mid 1960s, there was demand for an abundant labour force as a result of the booming plastic artificial flower business and other light industries in Hong Kong. Keung came up with the idea to outsource the assembly work to housewives; Yun and her husband were responsible to be the outpost of the factory for farming out the work. This was not an easy job, it took long working hours every day, but it was bringing a decent income for the family.

In 1967, Yun's oldest son Kwan Cheung (鈞祥) finished his secondary school and was employed by Keung's plastic artificial flower factory. Like his uncle Keung, Kwan Cheung was the eldest son and he took on the burden of earning a wage to support the family and younger siblings. There was a female co-worker by the name of Ngai Hau Shim (倪巧嬋), whom later married Kwan Cheung, so Keung's factory became the matchmaker for this couple.

Yun had kidney problems for more than thirty years before she died, yet she was a very courageous woman and lived her life with the help of dialysis for more than ten years. Yun lived in Taiwan for a couple of years around the turn of the Millennium because her third son Biu Cheung (彪祥) was a physician there. Sin and Karen visited Yun while she was living in Taiwan in year 2000, and Yun expressed her feelings to Sin that she was quite bored living in Hualin County because she could not speak Mandarin. The reason she was living there was because she had dialysis paid by the health insurance policy that her son bought for her. However, she later chose to return to Hong Kong because she wanted to be closer with her other children and grandchildren, but mainly because she could not understand Mandarin and the language barrier did not make her feel at home in Taiwan. In Hong Kong, she continued to have dialysis from the public hospital.

Ever since Yun passed away in 2008, Sin missed his sister every time he visited Hong Kong. Sin still has the memory of his sister Yun taking care of him when he was a young boy right after their father passed away in 1956. Without her care, Sin could possibly go astray on the streets of Sham Shui Po and wasted two of his critical schooling years. It made a difference to one's life when a guiding hand was there at the right place and at the right time.

CHAPTER TWELVE

Hong Kong Took Off in the Last Quarter of the 20th Century

W hen Sin went back to Hong Kong in 1974 for the first time since moving to Canada, the Hong Kong Mass Transit Railway (MTR) did not exist then. The construction of the MTR began in 1975, and the initial system opened in 1979. Today, the Hong Kong MTR is the most popular public transit option in Hong Kong. With the infrastructure of a mass transit system, land development was catching up to put affordable residential housing in areas much further away from the city. Shopping centres and restaurants were built close to the MTR stations, allowing commuters to spend more time shopping and dining before they went home at night. These conditions helped to fuel the local economic boom in Hong Kong.

Hong Kong was enjoying an unprecedented expansion during the last quarter of the 20th century. The success of manufacturing was the initial economic engine, and the factors that made Hong Kong successful were: the ability to provide labour-intensive manufacturing cheaper than the other developed countries; the entrepreneurship spirit of its people; and its flexibility in production. From 1971 to 1980, Hong Kong's industrial development extended into finance, tourism, real estate, transportation, and manufacturing began to diversify into electronics, watch, toys and jewellery industries[8].

Keung's business was also at its prime in the mid 1970s. In fact, he started to diversify his business back in the 1960s. In 1965, he and his plastic flower business partner, Mr. P.M. Leung, engaged in real estate development on Tung Choi Street in Mong Kok, Kowloon. And in 1966, Keung included another business partner, Mr. W.K. Tung into his toy manufacturing business. Keung's business now included plastic artificial flowers, plastic/polyester artificial flowers, toys, and real estate.

Due to immigrating to the U.S., Mr. P.M. Leung broke off the business partnership with Keung in 1967, so they agreed that Mr. Leung had ownership of the development on Tung Choi Street, while Keung took the ownership of the industrial unit at Wah Yuen Factory Building in Tai Kok Tsui. This left Keung with sole ownership of the plastic flower business. In 1977, his multi-storey factory building on Lei Muk Road in Kwai Chung was finally built on the piece of land which he had bought and held for a few years. He named the building Kentucky Industrial Building, after his factory, the Kentucky Plastic Works Limited. Finally, Keung had managed to put the name of his business on the map of Kwai Chung in Hong Kong, and this was a very significant achievement for him. The artificial flower factory and the toy factory were also relocated from Tai Kok Tsui to this building in Kwai Chung.

From the 1980s, the manufacturing sector in Hong Kong was gradually decreasing, while the service sector was increasing gradually. Again, Keung's business was right there and flexible enough to adjust for changes. Labour cost was creeping up slowing in Hong Kong, the demand for artificial flowers was waning, and so, in 1981 the operation of the artificial flower factory was seized. Later in 1985, Keung moved his toy production to a factory located in mainland China. The toy factory was in the town of Fenggang, which was in Dongguan prefecture, Guangdong province, China. While the toy manufacturing was doing well in China, the Hong Kong production capacity was reduced to a minimum to serve as a packaging and shipping facilities for the final products. Keung also invested in real estates in the town of Fenggang, China, where he set up the toy factory. Due to the nearby location of the Container Terminals in Kwai Chung, the industrial spaces in the Kentucky Industrial Building became hot demand for warehouse usage, and the real estate values went up as well. And so, before the turn of the Millennium and to realize the return on investment, Keung had gradually sold off most of the industrial spaces in the Kentucky Industrial Building.

It seemed obvious, and not coincident at all, that Keung's business was very much affected by the economic tides of Hong Kong. Or we can say that in business, if you stay the course and flow with the tides, you will survive the waves and turbulence along the ride. Keung not only survived the tides smartly, his business grew from a small factory into a cross-border enterprise.

CHAPTER THIRTEEN

The Golden Years

The sovereignty of Hong Kong was reverted back to China in 1997, officially ending 156 years of British Colonial rule, and became a special administrative region (SAR) of the People's Republic of China. After 1997, Keung's business was also affected by the economics of the times, first, the Asian financial crisis, and then secondly, the severe acute respiratory syndrome (SARS) outbreak in Hong Kong. Labour cost in Mainland China was not cheap like it used to be, it became harder and harder to operate the manufacturing in China and stay profitable. After Keung's first wife passed away due to cancer in 1981, he married his current wife, Linda, the mother of Raymond and Margaret. Six years later in 1987, Keung and his family immigrated to Australia but still maintained his business in Hong Kong and China.

In Australia, Keung bought a piece of secluded property near a golf course, torn down the original house on the lot and built a house on it between 1989 and 1990. The remaining land of the original lot was subdivided into three smaller lots in 1991 for future development. He had some property investments in Sydney but most of them have now been sold off. In Sydney, Keung had a business partner whom he had trusted and agreed to be his guarantor for a bank loan. But later, the loan was defaulted and the bank claimed losses from Keung. This was quite a misfortune for him, but he took the case to court and won it on the basis that his English was not good enough to have properly understood the legal contract.

While in Hong Kong, Foo was a loyal business partner of Keung. He made the sacrifice of commuting to and from his home in Hong Kong to work in China for more than twenty years. In 2003, Keung was approaching seventy years of age and decided to retire. However, things were turning for the worse due to the global economic meltdown of 2008, and Foo also decided in 2009 to retire by selling his share to the factory's management team-members. Foo and his family live in Hong Kong, and his adult children, Jackson and Benny (禮信, 禮邦) and daughter Freda (慧敏), are all married and living in Hong Kong. Foo and his wife Tse Gam Ching (謝鑑清) have three grandsons (嘉聰, 天佑, 朗軒).

After retiring from work, Keung chooses to live in Shenzhen, the neighbouring Chinese city just north of Hong Kong. His wife Linda, son Raymond and daughter-in-law Peggy live in Australia; his oldest daughter Wai Yu (慧茹) is married to Francis Weih and she and her family are living in Austria. Two of Keung's daughters, Wai Yan and Margaret (慧茵, 慧明) live in Hong Kong, daughter Joni (慧瓊) lives in Australia. His third daughter Jannix (慧嫻) is married to Kingsley Poon and they make their home in Canada. Keung has four grandchildren; grandson (Lee Weih) and granddaughter (Charito Weih) live in Austria, granddaughter Carol (daughter of Joni) lives in Australia, and granddaughter Hayley (daughter of Jannix) lives in Canada.

Yun had three surviving sons and three daughters (艷姬, 雯姬, 寶姬) when she passed away. Her eldest son Kwan Cheung (鈞祥) and youngest daughter (寶姬) live in the U.S.; third son Biu Cheung (彪祥) lives and practises medicine in Taiwan; middle daughter (雯姬) lives in the U.K.; and second eldest son Kok Cheung (國祥) and eldest daughter (艷姬) live in Hong Kong. Yun had four granddaughters (樂思, 韻思, 凱思, 翠詩) and six grandsons (進業, 宏業, 智業, 文豪, Wilson, Adam) who make their homes in the U.S., Taiwan, Hong Kong, Australia, and United Kingdom.

Sin took retirement after working as an engineer in Canada for 36 years[9]. His children and grand children are first and second generation Canadians. His son Felix (禮漢), and daughter Cindy (慧珊), are living in Toronto. Felix is married to Stephanie, and they are proud parents of Keira (煒然) and Keegan (朗然). Sin has made his home in Toronto Canada for many years, and he would not trade it for any other place in the world. Sin's new interest now is on the arts side, and his main passion in the last three years is to learn and play the two-stringed bowed musical instrument, called the *erhu* (二胡). He finds out from Keung that he is an erhu player too, and Sin wishes that they could play erhu together in his future visits to Hong Kong.

In the golden years of these three brothers, the moments being spent together reminiscing, talking and laughing about the past are precious. Sin is very grateful that his two brothers are in reasonable good health and enjoying their lives. Keung likes to talk about his struggle during his younger days and Sin thinks that these valuable experiences are worthy to be recorded. Sin is hoping to have more opportunities to travel to Hong Kong and spend more time with his brothers; to revisit the old schools he had attended and the old neighbourhood he was familiar with.

Sin feels that there is an unspoken respect towards his eldest brother. Keung can now look back at his achievements in life and feel proud of, not only the tangible wealth, but the intangible honour of being a dear brother to his siblings who feel profoundly indebted to his care and generosity towards them.

May the offsprings of the *Siblings* stay connected, and remember the story of this once struggling family. Love your parents because they did everything to raise you. Love and respect your brothers and sisters the way they are, exercise compassion and tolerance to them if they were not what you expect them to be.

Photo of Sin taken in 2007

REFERENCES

1. A renovated *tong lau* at 119-121 Nam Cheong Street. Photo courtesy of **Dr. Richard Wong Tai Choi** (黃棣才博士).

2. 137 Yee Kuk Street Sham Shui Po Public Dispensary. Photo courtesy of **Dr. Richard Wong Tai Choi** (黃棣才博士).

3. Shek Kip Mei Street St. Francis of Assisi Catholic Church. Photo courtesy of **Dr. Richard Wong Tai Choi** (黃棣才博士).

4. A *tong lau* at 181-183 Pei Ho Street. Photo courtesy of **Dr. Richard Wong Tai Choi** (黃棣才博士).

5. Street scene at 117-125 Nam Cheong Street. Photo courtesy of **Dr. Richard Wong Tai Choi** (黃棣才博士).

6. Photo of Foo, Keung, Shum Won To and daughter.

7. Photo of Sin and Wai Yu.

8. Hong Kong Economic History, Chen, C.Y., Assistant Professor, Division of Social Science, Hong Kong University of Science and Technology.

9. Photo of Sin taken in 2007.